O let us be married!

O let us be married!

THE OWL AND THE PUSSYCAT

KCP POETRY
An Imprint of Kids Can Press

VISIONS IN POETRY

EDWARD LEAR

The Owl and the Pussycat

with illustrations by STÉPHANE JORISCH

The **Owl** and the **Pussycat**
went to sea

In a beautiful **pea-green** boat,

They took some **honey**, and plenty of **money**, Wrapped up in a five-pound **note**.

The **Owl**
looked up to
the **stars** above,
And sang to a small
guitar,

"O lovely Pussy!
O Pussy,
my love,
What a beautiful
Pussy you are,
You are,
You are!
What a **beautiful**
Pussy you are!"

Pussy said to the Owl,
"You **elegant** fowl!
How charmingly
sweet you sing!

O let us be **married**!
Too long we have tarried:
But what shall we do for a **ring**?”

They sailed away,
for a **year**
and a **day**,

To the land where
the **Bong-tree** grows

And there in a wood
a **Piggy-wig** stood

With a **ring** at the end of his nose,
His nose,
His nose,
With a ring at the
end of his **nose**.

"Dear Pig,
are you willing
to sell for one shilling
Your **ring?"**

Said the Piggy,

"I will."

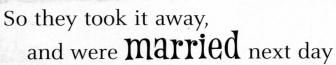

So they took it away,
and were **married** next day

By the **Turkey**
who lives on the **hill**.

They dined on mince,
and slices of **quince**,
Which they ate with a
runcible spoon;

And hand in hand,
on the edge of the sand,
They danced by the light
of the moon,

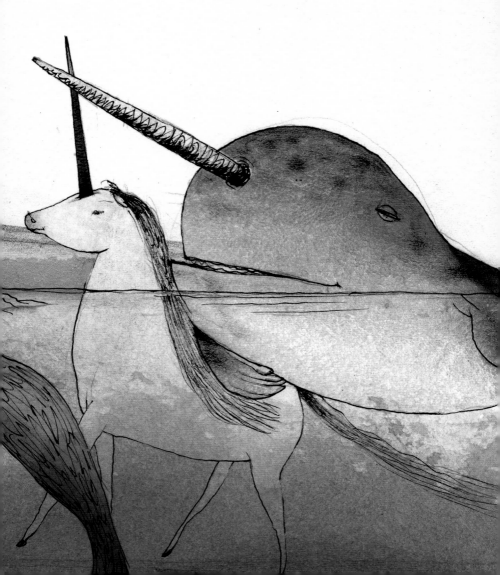

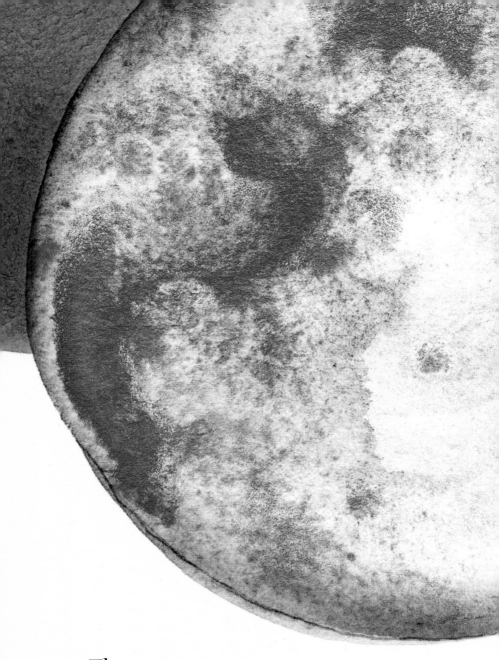

The moon,

The moon,

They danced

by the light of the moon.

Edward Lear

Edward Lear (1812–88) achieved renown as one of the Victorian masters of nonsense poetry. But Lear left behind more than a legacy of light verse: he was an accomplished nature and landscape artist as well as the author and illustrator of many travel books. Lear began his career as a zoological draftsman. At the age of 25, he left England, never to live there again, and traveled widely. One of Lear's illustrated journals of his wanderings caught the attention of Queen Victoria, who invited the artist to give her drawing lessons. Lear went on to publish a number of nonsense books for children, the first being a collection of limericks that popularized the form. Like the work of Lewis Carroll, his verse is well-known for its verbal inventiveness; however, what distinguishes Lear's nonsense is his lyrical style and his play with the sound of words rather than with their meaning. Despite its jovial surface, there is an undercurrent of melancholy in the poetry of Lear, which some have interpreted as a reflection of his personal struggles with loneliness and depression, epilepsy, bronchitis and, in later life, partial blindness.

Lear wrote and illustrated his most famous nonsense poem, "The Owl and the Pussycat," for the daughter of a friend in 1867. An enchanting ballad about a mismatched couple who elope and escape to a seaside paradise, it combines the romanticism of the Victorians with the absurdity of nursery rhymes. Comprised of imaginative words and memorable verses, the poem is also notable for its coinage of the term "runcible spoon," a spoon-shaped fork. "The Owl and the Pussycat" is a joyful celebration of love, yet one can detect a tinge of sorrow in the idea of eccentric creatures who must run away for their relationship to flourish — a critique, perhaps, of the repressiveness and absurdity Lear found in his own English society. It is this marriage of adult sophistication and childlike delight that makes Lear's verses resonate with young and old more than a century after they were composed. Indeed, unlike some Victorian writings, which can be remote and difficult for modern readers, Lear's poem sings to us today as sweetly and charmingly as the "elegant fowl" crooning to his love.

Stéphane Jorisch

For his whimsical yet thought-provoking interpretation of "The Owl and the Pussycat," Stéphane Jorisch looked beyond the fanciful text to Lear's own illustrations of the poem and noticed an interesting discrepancy between the lighthearted verse and the rather unhappy-looking title characters. It is in the emotional ambiguity of Lear's creation, along with the notion of a mismatched couple, that Jorisch found his primary inspiration — and a new way of seeing this oft-depicted classic. In this unique interpretation, two characters from different worlds, a wealthy owl and a pussycat from literally the "Other Side of the Tracks," fall in love. To escape the prying eyes and disapproval of the segregated society in which they live, the star-crossed lovers sail away to a beautiful utopia in which there are no boundaries to love — a place where unions between creatures of all different shapes, sizes and species are embraced and celebrated. It is only in this pastoral paradise that the owl and the pussycat find true freedom and acceptance; only here are they able to shed their masks for good and reveal their true selves. Jorisch transforms what has generally been perceived as a simple love story into a beautiful tale about tolerance and the love all human beings can experience if we embrace one another in our differences. At the same time, his playful and fantastic images (inspired by the illustrations of Lear himself, as well as the films of Fellini, the art of Miro and The Beatles' *Yellow Submarine*) perfectly capture the humor and levity of this delightful poem. A 21st-century French Canadian illustrator and a 19th-century English poet probably have as much in common as an owl and a pussycat, but like the famous feline and fowl that brought them together, theirs is a match made in heaven.

One of the most accomplished illustrators in Canada today, Stéphane Jorisch is a three-time winner of the Governor General's Award for Illustration, Canada's most prestigious literary award. His previous books include *Oma's Quilt*, *Suki's Kimono* and the highly acclaimed *Jabberwocky*, the first volume in the Visions in Poetry series. He lives in Montreal, Quebec, with his girlfriend and their three children.

For A_____

"If a dog_____

would h_____

The illustrations for this book were rendered in
pencil, ink, watercolor and Adobe Photoshop.

The text was set in

Celeste and Fanfare

✠

KCP Poetry is an imprint of Kids Can Press

Illustrations © 2007 Stéphane Jorisch

Kids Can Press acknowledges the financial support of the Government of
Ontario, through the Ontario Media Development Corporation's Ontario Book
Initiative; the Ontario Arts Council; the Canada Council for the Arts; and
the Government of Canada, through the BPIDP, for our publishing activity.

Published in Canada by   Published in the U.S. by
Kids Can Press Ltd.   Kids Can Press Ltd.
29 Birch Avenue   2250 Military Road
Toronto, ON M4V 1E2   Tonawanda, NY 14150

www.kidscanpress.com

Edited by Tara Walker
Designed by Karen Powers
Printed and bound in China

The hardcover edition of this book is smyth sewn casebound.
The paperback edition of this book is limp sewn with a drawn-on cover.

CM 07 0 9 8 7 6 5 4 3 2 1
CM PA 07 0 9 8 7 6 5 4 3 2 1

National Library of Canada Cataloguing in Publication Data

Lear, Edward, 1812–1888.

The owl and the pussycat / written by Edward Lear;
with illustrations by Stéphane Jorisch.

(Visions in poetry)
Poem.
ISBN 978-1-55337-828-0 (bound)
ISBN 978-1-55453-232-2 (pbk.)

1. Nonsense-verses, English. 2. Children's poetry, English.
I. Jorisch, Stéphane II. Title. III. Series.

PR4879.L2O85 2007   j821'.8   C2006-902262-3

Kids Can Press is a *corus*™ Entertainment company